The Complete Keto Diet for Beginners #2020

Affordable, Quick & Healthy Budget Friendly Recipes to Heal Your Body & Help You Lose Weight (How I Lose 30 Pounds in 21-Day)

Dr Maria Houter

Table of contents

Introduction

Are you trying to lose weight but haven't had any luck with the diet programs you've tried?

You might have dropped a few pounds with some of the diet programs you've tried, but after a while, the weight you've lost comes back, much to your frustration and dismay.

Don't worry.

Here's a diet program that can finally help you achieve long-term weight loss results that you want: the ketogenic diet.

Ketogenic is a type of low-carb diet that has been found effective in helping people shed unwanted pounds. Research has shown that a diet low in carbohydrates can efficiently contribute to weight loss.

Now since there are many other low-carb diets aside from the keto diet, it makes you want to ask this question: is keto more effective than other low carb diet programs?

In this book, you will find the answer that you are looking for.

This book discusses not only the basics and benefits of the ketogenic diet, but also provides countless recipes that will help you whip up healthy and delicious dishes as you go on your journey to a much slimmer you.

Not only will you be able to finally achieve the body you've always wanted, you can also enjoy a much healthier lifestyle, thanks to this diet.

So are you ready to get started?

Chapter 1: The Basics of Keto Diet

Before we get started in cooking delicious ketogenic recipes, let's get to know first more about the basics of the keto diet. This will help you understand the diet more thoroughly so that formulating a diet plan will be so much easier.

What is the Keto Diet?

So, first, what is the keto diet?

People refer to the keto diet in different ways—ketogenic, keto, low carb high fat diet, LCHP diet, and so on.

The simplest way to define this diet program is that it is high in fat, moderate in protein and low in carbohydrates.

The principle of this diet is to reduce the intake of carbohydrates while increasing intake of fat. This practice puts your body in ketosis, a metabolic condition where in the body is forced to burn fat for energy.

Carbohydrates are commonly found in rice, bread, pasta, sugary treats and sugary beverages. When you're in a keto diet, you will be recommended to eat foods that are higher in protein and fats as well as vegetables.

How is Keto Different from Other Diets?

There are more low-carb diet programs than most people are aware of.

Here are some of the most popular ones with information on how each one works. This way, you can see the difference between keto and other low carb diet plans.

Atkins Diet

The Atkins Diet was introduced in the early 1970s by Dr. Robert Atkins. He published his research studies in a book titled Dr. Atkin's Diet Revolution. At present, there are two types of Atkins Diet: 20 and 40. In the Atkins 20 Diet Plan, the dieter will consume 20 to 100 grams net carbohydrates daily. In the 40 method, the dieter will take in net carbs of 40 to 100.

There are plenty foods that are avoided by dieters using this program, which is why supplements are recommended by experts.

Bulletproof Diet

The Bulletproof diet was developed by a blogger named Dave Asprey a few years ago. The purpose of this diet is not only to help people shed pounds but also to increase energy levels, mental stimulation and immunity. It recommends intake of 50 to 70 percent fats, 20 percent protein and 25 percent carbs.

In this program, the foods are divided into three colors: red, yellow and green. Green, which is similar to the traffic light go, includes foods that you are free to eat anytime you like. Yellow foods are those that you have to consume moderately. Foods in the red category should be avoided at all costs.

Dukan Diet

The Dukan diet is another low-carb diet. But this one is also low in fat. It requires higher protein intake than the keto diet. This is a highly restrictive diet that consists only of 100 foods. Nearly 70 of these are proteins and only 30 are from vegetables (non-starchy).

The Paleo Diet

The Paleo diet was invented by a physician named Loren Cordain. The concept of this diet is to consume only foods that were eaten by your ancestors during the prehistoric times. This is otherwise known as the caveman's diet. Any food product that has been processed or considered unnatural is off-limits. This is a highly restrictive diet that eliminates many types of foods including all types of grains.

Zero Carb Diet

The Zero Carb diet was introduced in the 1990s by an explored named Vilhjalmur Stefansson. He came about this diet program after residing in the Inuit tribe for years. The diet consisted mainly of fish and meat, and occasionally a few berries during summertime. Up to 95 percent of calories are from proteins and fats. The only carbs you will take in are from the meat glycogen.

What Makes the Keto Diet Program different?

Each of the diet program mentioned above shared some similarities with the keto diet—most encouraged lower intake of carbs as well as recommended natural and whole foods.

But the main difference is that the keto diet is backed by scientific research. Some of the diet programs mentioned above like the Bulletproof and the Zero Carb diets lack in scientific proof.

Another difference is the restriction. Some of the diets discussed above are too restrictive that many fails during the first few months. The Paleo diet for example eliminates all types of grains that it can be quite hard to adjust especially if you are fond of eating rice, pasta or bread.

How Does the Ketogenic Diet Work?

The term "keto" comes from "ketones".

To get energy, the body burns the carbohydrates that you take in while storing the fats in your bodily tissue.

So when you take in less carbs and more fats, the body is forced to burn the fat instead because it runs out of carbs to burn.

When the body burns fat for energy, it puts the body in a state referred to as "ketosis".

During this state, the body produces a by-product called "ketones", and this is where the diet is named after.

Ketones are produced by the body when you consume fewer carbs and moderate protein. These are produced in the liver, and are used as energy source not only by the body but also by the brain.

Since the body no longer stores fat in your tissues but instead burns them, the result is weight loss.

How to Know When You are in Ketosis

There are various ways of finding out when you've reached the state of ketosis. One is through the signs and side effects.

Here are some signs that you have reached this state:

- Dry mouth
- Metallic taste inside the mouth
- Frequent thirst
- Frequent urination
- Bad breath

- Lethargy
- Reduced appetite

Another way is by measuring ketones inside your body. There are three devices that you can use to measure ketone levels:

- Urine strips
- Breath analyzers
- Blood meter

The simplest way to measure ketones is by using a urine strip. This is also the cheapest option, which is why this is commonly preferred by beginners. Simply dip the device in your urine and the strip will change in color. If you have high ketone levels, the strip will turn into dark purple.

You can also make use of a ketone breath analyzer or a blood ketone meter. The blood meter is the most accurate way of measuring ketone levels, but is also the most expensive option.

It's also possible to experience side effects during the first few days of undergoing the keto diet, and these include:

- Cramps
- Constipation
- Headache
- Fatigue
- Irritability
- Lightheadedness

These side effects may or may not indicate that you have reached the state of ketosis, but are commonly experienced by those who are starting out with the diet. These usually go away after a few days or weeks.

The Health Benefits of Keto Diet

The keto diet wouldn't have become popular if it were not highly beneficial. Users attest of the high efficacy of this diet program, claiming that they lose significant amount of weight only a few weeks after starting.

Here are the many benefits that are linked to the keto diet:

- Curbs the appetite

One of the most common problems among people who are trying to lose weight is the hunger pangs. When you feel hungry, it becomes hard to resist food, and follow your diet plan. It's so easy to get tempted and to devour foods that are not included in your program. But the good news is that when you're on a keto diet, you don't experience as many hunger pangs or cravings as before. Research has proven that the ketosis effectively suppresses the appetite. Keto dieters feel full longer than people who are on regular diet.

- Helps drop unwanted pounds

It has been mentioned over and over how the keto diet helps people lose weight, and it is through increased burning of fat in the body. It is also through appetite suppression as well as through reduction in the levels of insulin.

- Normalizes blood sugar and insulin levels

This is the reason that people suffering from diabetes are recommended to adopt this diet program. In fact, it has been found in some studies that people who are on a keto diet can discontinue their intake of diabetes medication.

- Enhances physical endurance

It has been shown in research that ketosis can also provide lasting energy levels even during sustained physical workouts. While it's true that you will at first experience fatigue and lethargy, once the body adjusts and gets used to the new diet, you will enjoy the higher levels of energy.

- Manages seizure

Ketogenic diet was originally designed to reduce seizure attacks among people who have epilepsy. This has been proven highly effective not only in adults but also in children. In fact, those who do not respond well to anti-seizure medicines find this diet effective in managing their condition.

Other benefits of the keto diet include:

- Minimizing severity and frequency of headaches due to migraine
- Reversing the polycystic ovary syndrome
- Slowing down the progress of Alzheimer's disease

8 Helpful Tips for the Keto Journey

To help you succeed in your journey with the ketogenic diet, here are some pointers to remember:

Tip # 1 – Minimize stress

Some people find it hard to reach ketosis. One possible reason is stress.

When the body is stressed, the cortisol hormone also known as the "stress hormone" increases the levels of blood sugar in the body. This hinders the body's ability to burn fats. If you want to reach ketosis more quickly, minimize the stressors in your life. You should also turn to stress reduction techniques such as breathing exercises, meditation, yoga and massage. Even reading a book or listening to soothing music can do wonders for you.

Tip # 2 – Get enough sleep

Sleep deprivation is just as bad as stress. Lack of sleep also increases cortisol in the body, preventing your body's fat burning process. Make sure that you get enough sleep at night. Try to sleep at the same hour each night to establish your bedtime routine.

Tip # 3 – Take in more salt

When the body has lower insulin levels, it excretes a higher amount of salt. This is why, keto dieters are advised to add between 3,000 and 5,000 milligrams of sodium in your diet. But of course, you have to do this the healthy way.

Some pointers to remember:

- Use sea salt
- Drink organic bone broth several times a week
- Eat foods that contain sodium such as celery or salted walnuts

Tip # 4 – Get more exercise

It is imperative for keto dieters to exercise more. This helps you make a smoother transition to your diet. As mentioned earlier, lethargy is a common side effect during the first few weeks of starting this diet. Exercise can counter this unpleasant side effect.

Tip # 5 – Avoid diet soda

In the list of foods and drinks to avoid, you will find sugary beverages like soda. This might make you think that it's acceptable to replace it with diet soda. But it's not. Diet soda may not have any calories but it's also off-limits for keto dieters. This increases cravings for sweet drinks and foods.

Tip # 6 – Cook in batches

This tip works well not only among keto dieters, but for anyone who's starting any type of weight loss diet. When you're on a diet, it becomes hard to sometimes track what you're eating. There are also times when you will feel tempted to veer away from your diet. When you cook meals in batches, you make it easier for yourself to resist temptations. It's also more efficient this way.

Tip # 7 – Stay hydrated

Frequent thirst is a common side effect among keto dieters. This is why it's very important to stay hydrated by drinking plenty of fluids daily. Make sure that you drink at least half of your weight in fluid ounces.

Tip # 8 – Be patient

Starting a new diet is never easy. Don't be too hard on yourself. Be patient because it will take a while before you can get adjusted to a new diet.

Chapter 2: Foods to Eat

Here's a quick list of all foods and drinks that you can eat while on the keto diet:

- Meat – Preferably unprocessed, organic, and grass-fed meat
- Fish and seafood – Go for fatty fish such as salmon
- Eggs – Buy organic eggs
- Fats – Use natural and healthy fats (olive oil, butter, coconut oil)
- Low-carb vegetables – Cabbage, avocado, zucchini, cauliflower, broccoli
- Salt, pepper, herbs and spices
- High fat dairy – Butter, yogurts, heavy cream
- Nuts – Pecan, macadamia, and low-carb nuts
- Berries – Strawberries, blackberries, blueberries, cherries
- Water
- Coffee – Coffee with little cream or milk but no sugar
- Tea – Black, green, herbal tea
- Broth – Chicken broth, beef broth, vegetable broth, bone broth

Chapter 3: Foods to Avoid

When it comes to foods and drinks to avoid, here are those that you should stay away from:

- High carb foods – Pasta, bread, rice, grains
- Sugary foods and beverages– All sodas, soft drinks, fruit juice, sports drinks, breakfast cereals, and regular desserts such as cakes, cookies, sweets, chocolate bars, donuts, candies (keto-friendly desserts such as those in the desserts recipe section are allowed)
- Sugar and other sweet condiments – Honey, agave and maple syrup
- Starchy vegetables – Potatoes, sweet potatoes and products made from these vegetables (potato chips, French fries)
- Legumes – Lentils and beans
- Fruits
- Margarine

Chapter 4: FAQs

FAQ # 1 – Is keto a fad diet?

This is one of the most common questions asked by people who have no idea how the keto diet works. But if you'll look at the scientific proof, you'll see that it is different from other fat diet programs because it produces long-term results.

FAQ # 2 – How much weight can I lose after I start this diet?

It is hard to determine the exact weight that you will lose but most people claim that they lose up to 4 pounds in the first week. Some people lose 1 pound after that. It has been found that men lose weight more quickly than women.

FAQ # 3 – Should I take in supplements while on the keto diet?

Unlike with other diet programs, you are not required to take in any type of supplements while on the ketogenic diet program.

FAQ # 4 – Can I use artificial sweeteners?

You are only allowed to use sugar alternatives that are indicated as keto-friendly. Just one example is stevia.

FAQ # 5 – Is the keto diet safe?

Generally, the keto diet is safe but it's imperative to know that it is not for everyone. Ketogenic diet is not recommended for people who have high blood pressure, women who are pregnant or lactating, or people with serious ailments.

It is very important that you first consult your doctor before undergoing this diet program.

Chapter 5: 30-Day Meal Plan

Day 1

Breakfast: Baked Eggs with Hollandaise Sauce

Lunch: Greek Meatballs

Dinner: Crab Salad

Day 2

Breakfast: Hot Choco

Lunch: Tuscan Pork

Dinner: Lemon & Butter Shrimp

Day 3

Breakfast: Breakfast Salad

Lunch: Slow Cooked Lamb Shanks

Dinner: Salmon Patties

Day 4

Breakfast: Breakfast Porridge

Lunch: Grilled Lemon Chicken

Dinner: Buffalo Cauliflower

Day 5

Breakfast: Breakfast Muffins

Lunch: Greek Meatballs

Dinner: Coconut Shrimp

Day 6

Breakfast: Sausage & Egg Breakfast

Sandwich

Lunch: Chicken Curry

Dinner: Buffalo Cauliflower

Day 7

Breakfast: Breakfast Bowl

Lunch: Tuscan Pork

Dinner: Herbed Salmon

Day 8

Breakfast: Cabbage Hash Browns

Lunch: Chicken in Creamy Lemon Garlic Sauce

Dinner: Beef Tagliata

Day 9

Breakfast: Baked Egg & Blueberries

Lunch: Clam Chowder

Dinner: Baked Cod & Asparagus

Day 10

Breakfast: Breakfast Energizing Smoothie

Lunch: Baked Cajun Chicken

Dinner: Garlic & Rosemary Lamb

Day 11

Breakfast: Breakfast Salad

Lunch: Lemon & Butter Shrimp

Dinner: Trout in Dill Cream Sauce

Day 12

Breakfast: Breakfast Steak & Eggs

Lunch: Salmon in Creamy Tomato Sauce

Dinner: Korean Beef

Day 13

Breakfast: Breakfast Muffins

Lunch: Spicy Chicken Wings

Dinner: Crab Salad

Day 14

Breakfast: Asparagus Frittata

Lunch: Beef Egg Roll Slaw

Dinner: Buffalo Cauliflower

Day 15

Breakfast: Baked Eggs with Hollandaise Sauce

Lunch: Slow Cooked Lamb Shanks

Dinner: Spicy Chicken Fritters

Day 16

Breakfast: Breakfast Skillet

Lunch: Barbecue Chicken

Dinner: Salmon with Basil & Avocado

Day 17

Breakfast: Hot Choco

Lunch: Clam Chowder

Dinner: Tuna Salad

Day 18

Breakfast: Keto Cereal

Lunch: Beef Egg Roll Slaw

Dinner: Salmon Patties

Day 19

Breakfast: Breakfast Bowl

Lunch: Baked Chicken

Dinner: Grilled Shrimp Kebab

Day 20

Breakfast: Breakfast Porridge

Lunch: Bacon Cheeseburger Casserole

Dinner: Vegetable Medley with Bacon Bits

Day 21

Breakfast: Sausage & Egg Breakfast Sandwich

Lunch: Lemon & Butter Shrimp

Dinner: Garlic & Rosemary Lamb

Day 22

Breakfast: Breakfast Energizing Smoothie

Lunch: Pork Belly Cracklings

Dinner: Grilled Lemon Chicken

Day 23

Breakfast: Cabbage Hash Browns

Lunch: Baked Cod & Asparagus

Dinner: Greek Meatballs

Day 24

Breakfast: Breakfast Skillet

Lunch: Tuna Salad

Dinner: Baked Cajun Chicken

Day 25

Breakfast: Asparagus Frittata

Lunch: Salmon in Creamy Tomato Sauce

Dinner: Chicken Strips

Day 26

Breakfast: Baked Egg & Blueberries

Lunch: Bacon Salad

Dinner: Trout in Dill Cream Sauce

Day 27

Breakfast: Breakfast Steak & Eggs

Lunch: Lamb Chops with Herb Butter

Dinner: Grilled Lemon Chicken

Day 28

Breakfast: Keto Cereal

Lunch: Salmon in Creamy Tomato Sauce

Dinner: Tuscan Pork

Day 29

Breakfast: Egg & Zucchini Cups

Lunch: Crab Salad

Dinner: Garlic Chicken

Day 30

Breakfast: Bacon & Cheese Omelette

Lunch: Coconut Shrimp

Dinner: Beef Egg Roll Slaw

Chapter 6: Breakfast

Breakfast Energizing Smoothie

Preparation Time: 10 minutes
Cooking Time: 10 minutes
Servings: 2

Ingredients:

- ¼ cup almond milk
- ¾ cup coconut milk
- ½ avocado, sliced
- ½ teaspoon turmeric
- 1 teaspoon ginger, grated
- 1 teaspoon freshly squeezed lemon juice
- 1 cup ice

Method:

1. Add all the ingredients in a blender.
2. Blend until smooth.

Nutritional Value:

- Calories 232
- Total Fat 22.4 g
- Saturated Fat 10 g
- Cholesterol 50 mg
- Sodium 25 mg
- Total Carbohydrate 6 g
- Dietary Fiber 2.8 g
- Protein 10 g
- Total Sugars 1.1 g
- Potassium 561 mg

Breakfast Salad

Preparation Time: 10 minutes
Cooking Time: 0 minute
Servings: 2

Ingredients:

- 3 cups kale, shredded
- 2 teaspoons olive oil
- 1 teaspoon red wine vinegar
- Salt to taste
- 2 oz. avocado, sliced
- 2 eggs, hard boiled and sliced into wedges
- 10 cherry tomatoes, sliced in half
- 4 strips bacon, cooked and chopped

Method:

1. Toss the kale in the mixture of oil, vinegar and salt.
2. Let sit until kale has softened.
3. Arrange in serving bowls and top with the rest of the ingredients.

Nutritional Value:

- Calories 292
- Total Fat 18 g
- Saturated Fat 4.5 g
- Cholesterol 191 mg
- Sodium 335.5 mg
- Total Carbohydrate 8 g
- Dietary Fiber 5 g
- Protein 17 g
- Total Sugars 2 g
- Potassium 670 mg

Baked Eggs with Hollandaise Sauce

Preparation Time: 10 minutes
Cooking Time: 20 minutes
Servings: 4

Ingredients:

- 4 oz. bacon, chopped
- ½ cup kale, shredded
- ½ cup spinach, chopped
- ½ cup dairy-free and keto-friendly Hollandaise sauce

Method:

1. Preheat your oven to 400 degrees F.
2. Cook the bacon in a pan over medium heat.
3. Cook until golden and crispy.
4. Stir in the kale and spinach.
5. Cook until the greens have wilted.
6. Transfer mixture into heatproof ramekins.
7. Crack eggs into each ramekin.
8. Bake in the oven for 10 to 15 minutes.
9. Serve with the hollandaise sauce.

Nutritional Value:

- Calories 166
- Total Fat 12.1g
- Saturated Fat 3.9g
- Cholesterol 31mg
- Sodium 717mg
- Total Carbohydrate 2.8g
- Dietary Fiber 0.2g
- Protein 11.2g
- Total Sugars 0g
- Potassium 230mg

Asparagus Frittata

Preparation Time: 10 minutes
Cooking Time: 20 minutes
Servings: 4

Ingredients:

- 1 tablespoon olive oil
- 2 teaspoons butter
- ½ lb. asparagus, trimmed and sliced
- 8 eggs, beaten
- 7 tablespoons almond milk
- Salt and pepper to taste
- ½ cup Parmesan cheese, grated

Method:

1. Pour the olive oil into a pan over medium heat.
2. Cook the asparagus for 10 minutes. Stir occasionally.
3. In a bowl, mix the eggs, milk, salt, pepper and Parmesan cheese.
4. Add the mixture into the pan.
5. Cook for 10 minutes.
6. Serve the frittata inverted on a plate.

Nutritional Value:

- Calories 242
- Total Fat 17.6g
- Saturated Fat 7.0g
- Cholesterol 344mg
- Sodium 342mg
- Total Carbohydrates 4.6g
- Dietary Fiber 1.2g
- Protein 17.1g
- Total Sugars 3g
- Potassium 291mg

Sausage & Egg Breakfast Sandwich

Preparation Time: 5 minutes
Cooking Time: 15 minutes
Servings: 3

Ingredients:

- 6 eggs
- 2 tablespoons heavy cream
- Salt and pepper to taste
- 1 tablespoon butter
- 3 slices cheddar cheese
- 6 sausage patties, cooked
- ½ avocado, sliced

Method:

1. Beat the eggs in a bowl.
2. Stir in the cream, salt and pepper.
3. Add the butter to a pan over medium heat.
4. Add 1/3 of the eggs into the pan.
5. Place the cheese in the center.
6. Cook for 1 minute.
7. Fold the sides to cover the cheese.
8. Do the same for the remaining eggs.
9. Place the egg with cheese on top of a sausage patty.
10. Top with the avocado slice.
11. Top with another sausage patty.
12. Repeat the steps to make a total of three breadless sandwiches.

Nutritional Value:

- Calories 554
- Total Fat 45.6g
- Saturated Fat 18.4g
- Cholesterol 446mg
- Sodium 690mg
- Total Carbohydrate 4.2g
- Dietary Fiber 2.3g
- Total Sugars 1g
- Protein 32.1g
- Potassium 476mg

Breakfast Bowl

Preparation Time: 10 minutes
Cooking Time: 15 minutes
Serving: 1

Ingredients:

- 1 teaspoon olive oil
- 1 onion, sliced
- 6 mushrooms, sliced
- ½ cup ground beef
- ½ teaspoon smoked paprika
- Salt and pepper to taste
- 2 eggs, beaten
- ½ avocado, diced
- 10 black olives, pitted and sliced

Method:

1. Pour the oil into a pan over medium heat.
2. Cook the onion and mushrooms for 2 minutes.
3. Add the ground beef and cook for 5 minutes.
4. Season with paprika, salt and pepper.
5. Transfer to a plate.
6. Add the eggs and cook until firm on the sides.
7. Arrange the beef, avocado, eggs and olives in a bowl.

Nutritional Value:

- Calories 571
- Total Fat 40.9g
- Saturated Fat 9.2g
- Cholesterol 365mg
- Sodium 552mg
- Total Carbohydrate 16.5g
- Dietary Fiber 12g
- Total Sugars 7.8g
- Protein 31g
- Potassium 1310mg

Breakfast Muffins

Preparation Time: 15 minutes
Cooking Time: 25 minutes
Servings: 2

Ingredients:

- 1 teaspoon coconut oil
- 2 cups spinach, chopped
- 2 tablespoons basil, chopped
- 6 strips bacon, cooked and chopped
- 10 eggs
- ½ teaspoon garlic powder
- Salt and pepper to taste

Method:

1. Preheat your oven to 350 degrees F.
2. Grease your muffin pan with coconut oil.
3. In a pan over medium heat, add a little coconut oil.
4. Heat it through and then cook the spinach for 1 minute.
5. Remove from the stove.
6. Stir in the basil and bacon.
7. In another bowl, beat the eggs.
8. Season the eggs with garlic powder, salt and pepper.
9. Transfer bacon mixture into the muffin cups.
10. Add the egg mixture on top.
11. Bake in the oven for 20 minutes.

Nutritional Value:

- Calories 653
- Total Fat 48.1g
- Saturated Fat 16.6g
- Cholesterol 881mg
- Sodium 1649mg
- Total Carbohydrate 4.2g
- Dietary Fiber 0.8g
- Protein 49.9g
- Total Sugars 2g
- Potassium 800mg

Breakfast Skillet

Preparation Time: 10 minutes
Cooking Time: 13 minutes
Servings: 4

Ingredients:

- 1 lb. ground pork
- 8 oz. mushrooms, chopped
- 2 zucchini, sliced
- Salt and pepper to taste
- ½ teaspoon basil
- ½ teaspoon garlic powder
- 2 tablespoons Dijon mustard

Method:

1. Pour the oil into a pan over medium heat.
2. Cook the mushrooms for 4 minutes.
3. Add the zucchini and cook for 4 minutes.
4. Season with salt and pepper.
5. Push the mushrooms and zucchini to the sides.
6. Add the ground pork in the middle of the pan.
7. Season with the basil and garlic powder.
8. Cook for 5 minutes.
9. Stir everything including the Dijon mustard.

Nutritional Value:

- Calories 196
- Total Fat 4.6g
- Saturated Fat 1.4g
- Cholesterol 83mg
- Sodium 166mg
- Total Carbohydrate 5.8g
- Dietary Fiber 2g
- Total Sugars 2.8g
- Protein 33.1g
- Potassium 930mg

Breakfast Steak & Eggs

Preparation Time: 10 minutes
Cooking Time: 5 minutes
Serving: 1

Ingredients:

- 1 tablespoon butter
- 3 eggs
- 4 oz. sirloin beef
- Salt and pepper to taste
- ¼ avocado, sliced

Method:

1. Add the butter to a pan over medium heat.
2. Cook the eggs until yolks and whites are set.
3. Sprinkle with salt and pepper.
4. Transfer to a plate.
5. Add the sirloin and cook for 2 to 3 minutes per side.
6. Slice the steak.
7. Season with salt and pepper.
8. Serve steak with eggs and avocado.

Nutritional Value:

- Calories 510
- Total Fat 36 g
- Saturated Fat 15 g
- Cholesterol 49 mg
- Sodium 28 mg
- Total Carbohydrate 3 g
- Dietary Fiber 1 g
- Protein 44 g
- Total Sugars 1 g
- Potassium 670 mg

Breakfast Porridge

Preparation Time: 2 minutes
Cooking Time: 5 minutes
Serving: 1

Ingredients:

- ¾ cup water
- 2 tablespoons golden flax meal
- 2 tablespoons coconut flour
- Salt to taste
- 1 egg, beaten
- 2 teaspoons ghee
- 1 tablespoon coconut milk
- 1 tablespoons sweetener

Method:

1. Pour water into a pot over medium heat.
2. Stir in the golden flax meal, flour and salt.
3. Simmer until it has thickened.
4. Stir in the egg, ghee, coconut milk and sweetener.
5. Cook for 30 seconds.

Nutritional Value:

- Calories 345
- Total Fat 28.5 g
- Saturated Fat 13 g
- Cholesterol 232 mg
- Sodium 31 mg
- Total Carbohydrate 13 g
- Dietary Fiber 9 g
- Protein 13 g
- Total Sugars 1.4 g
- Potassium 550 mg

Baked Egg & Blueberries

Preparation Time: 10 minutes
Cooking Time: 20 minutes
Servings: 4

Ingredients:

- Cooking spray
- 1 tablespoon butter
- 5 eggs
- 3 tablespoons coconut flour
- ¼ teaspoon vanilla
- 1 teaspoon ginger, grated
- 1 teaspoon orange zest
- Salt to taste
- 1 teaspoon fresh rosemary, chopped
- ½ cup blueberries

Method:

1. Preheat your oven to 350 degrees F.
2. Grease your ramekins with cooking spray.
3. Put all the ingredients except the blueberries and rosemary in a blender.
4. Blend until smooth.
5. Stir in the rosemary and blend for a few seconds.
6. Pour the mixture into the ramekins.
7. Place the blueberries on top.
8. Bake for 20 minutes.

Nutritional Value:

- Calories 144
- Total Fat 15 g
- Saturated Fat 9 g
- Cholesterol 288 mg
- Sodium 22 mg
- Total Carbohydrate 2 g
- Dietary Fiber 0 g
- Protein 8.5 g
- Total Sugars 1 g
- Potassium 560 mg

Hot Choco

Preparation Time: 5 minutes
Cooking Time: 10 minutes
Servings: 1

Ingredients:

- 1 ¼ cups water, divided
- 2 tablespoons cocoa powder
- 2 ½ teaspoon keto sweetener
- ¼ cup heavy cream

Method:

1. Pour 2 tablespoons of water into a small pot over medium heat.
2. Stir in the cocoa and sweetener until dissolved.
3. Pour in the rest of the water.
4. Increase heat to medium high and stir in the cream.
5. Cook for 30 seconds.
6. Serve immediately.

Nutritional Value:

- Calories 127
- Total Fat 12.5g
- Saturated Fat 7.8g
- Cholesterol 41mg
- Sodium 22mg
- Total Carbohydrate 6.8g
- Dietary Fiber 3.2g
- Protein 2.6g
- Total Sugars 0.2g
- Potassium 296mg

Keto Cereal

Preparation Time: 10 minutes
Cooking Time: 25 minutes
Servings: 3

Ingredients:

- Cooking spray
- 1 cup coconut flakes (unsweetened)
- 1 cup walnuts, chopped
- 1 cup almonds, chopped
- 2 tablespoons flax seeds
- ¼ cup sesame seeds
- 2 tablespoons chia seeds
- 1 teaspoon vanilla
- ½ teaspoon ground clove
- 1 ½ teaspoon ground cinnamon
- Salt to taste
- ¼ cup coconut oil
- 1 egg white

Method:

1. Preheat your oven to 350 degrees F.
2. Coat your baking pan with cooking spray.
3. In a bowl, add all the ingredients except oil and egg white.
4. Mix well.
5. In another bowl, beat the egg.
6. Stir in the egg and oil into the granola.
7. Pour the mixture into the pan.
8. Bake for 25 minutes.
9. Let cool before serving.

Nutritional Value:

- Calories 399
- Total Fat 37.5g
- Saturated Fat 13.6g
- Cholesterol 0mg

- Sodium 38mg
- Total Carbohydrate 10.3g
- Dietary Fiber 6.3g
- Total Sugars 1.9g
- Protein 10.9g
- Potassium 334mg

Cabbage Hash Browns

Preparation Time: 10 minutes
Cooking Time: 20 minutes
Servings: 2

Ingredients:

- 2 eggs
- Salt and pepper to taste
- ½ teaspoon garlic powder
- ¼ onion, sliced
- 2 cups cabbage, shredded
- 1 tablespoon olive oil

Method:

1. In a bowl, beat the eggs and season with salt, pepper and garlic powder.
2. Toss the onion and cabbage into the egg mixture.
3. Pour the oil into a pan over medium heat.
4. Add the mixture to the pan and cook in batches for 3 to 4 minutes per side.

Nutritional Value:

- Calories 148
- Total Fat 11.5g
- Saturated Fat 2.4g
- Cholesterol 164mg
- Sodium 75mg
- Total Carbohydrate 6.2g
- Dietary Fiber 2.1g
- Protein 6.7g
- Total Sugars 3.3g
- Potassium 206mg

Egg & Zucchini Cups

Preparation Time: 15 minutes
Cooking Time: 30 minutes
Servings: 12

Ingredients:

- Cooking spray
- 2 zucchini, sliced with peeler
- ½ cup tomatoes, chopped
- ¼ lb. ham, cooked and chopped
- 8 eggs
- 1 cup cheddar cheese, shredded
- ½ cup heavy cream
- ½ teaspoon dried oregano
- Salt and pepper to taste

Method:

1. Preheat your oven to 400 degrees F.
2. Spray your muffin pan with oil.
3. Add the zucchini strips in each muffin cup, forming the crust.
4. Add the tomatoes and ham into each cup.
5. In a bowl, beat the eggs and stir in the rest of the ingredients.
6. Pour the egg mixture into the cups.
7. Bake for 30 minutes.

Nutritional Value:

- Calories 120
- Total Fat 8.8g
- Saturated Fat 4.4g
- Cholesterol 131mg
- Sodium 228mg
- Total Carbohydrate 2.3g
- Dietary Fiber 0.6g
- Total Sugars 1.1g
- Protein 8.2g
- Potassium 184mg

Chapter 7: Appetizers & Snacks

Baked Chicken Wings

Preparation Time: 1 hour and 10 minutes
Cooking Time: 1 hour
Servings: 5

Ingredients:

- 10 chicken wings
- 1 tablespoon baking powder
- Salt to taste
- Olive oil

Method:

1. Preheat your oven to 250 degrees F.
2. Dry chicken wings with paper towel.
3. Season with salt.
4. Let sit for 1 hour.
5. Season baking powder with a pinch of salt.
6. Coat chicken wings with baking powder.
7. Drizzle with oil.
8. Put on the baking pan.
9. Bake for 30 minutes.
10. Increase temperature to 450 degrees.
11. Bake for another 30 minutes.

Nutritional Value:

- Calories 161
- Total Fat 14 g
- Saturated Fat 8 g
- Cholesterol 22 mg
- Sodium 285 mg
- Total Carbohydrate 3 g
- Dietary Fiber 1 g
- Protein 10 g
- Total Sugars 0 g
- Potassium 310 mg

Cauliflower Sticks

Preparation Time: 20 minutes
Cooking Time: 30 minutes
Servings: 12

Ingredients:

- 6 cups cauliflower florets
- ½ cup mozzarella cheese, shredded
- ½ cup Parmesan cheese, grated
- ½ cup cheddar cheese, shredded
- 1 egg, beaten
- 1 clove garlic, minced
- ¼ cup fresh parsley, chopped
- ¼ cup fresh basil, chopped
- Salt and pepper to taste

Method:

1. Preheat your oven to 425 degrees F.
2. Add cauliflower in the food processor.
3. Pulse until finely ground.
4. Put in a heatproof bowl and microwave for 8 minutes.
5. Let cool and then squeeze with paper towel.
6. Take half of the cheeses and mix together in a bowl.
7. Stir in the rest of the ingredients in the bowl.
8. Flatten the mixture on a baking pan.
9. Bake for 20 minutes.
10. Sprinkle the remaining cheeses and bake for another 10 minutes.
11. Slice into sticks and serve with keto-friendly dip.

Nutritional Value:

- Calories 166
- Total Fat 18 g
- Saturated Fat 9 g
- Cholesterol 26 mg
- Sodium 340 mg
- Total Carbohydrate 4 g
- Dietary Fiber 1 g
- Protein 5 g
- Total Sugars 1 g
- Potassium 504 mg

Buffalo Chicken Strips

Preparation Time: 10 minutes
Cooking Time: 30 minutes
Servings: 6

Ingredients:

- 1 lb. chicken breast fillet, sliced into strips
- Salt and pepper to taste
- 1 cup almond flour
- 1 egg, beaten
- 1 tablespoon whipping cream
- 6 oz. buffalo sauce

Method:

1. Preheat your oven to 350 degrees F.
2. Season chicken with salt and pepper.
3. Sprinkle a little salt and pepper into the flour and mix well.
4. Mix the egg and cream.
5. Dip the chicken strip into the egg mixture and coat with flour.
6. Bake in the oven for 30 minutes.
7. Toss in the buffalo sauce.

Nutritional Value:

- Calories 323
- Total Fat 14.2g
- Saturated Fat 4.5g
- Cholesterol 195mg
- Sodium 152mg
- Total Carbohydrate 0.3g
- Dietary Fiber 0g
- Total Sugars 0.1g
- Protein 45.7g
- Potassium 392mg

Onion Rings

Preparation Time: 15 minutes
Cooking Time: 15 minutes
Servings: 2

Ingredients:

- 1 white onion, sliced into rings
- ½ cup coconut flour
- 2 eggs
- 1 tablespoon heavy whipping cream
- 2 oz. pork rinds
- ½ cup Parmesan cheese, grated

Method:

1. Prepare three bowls.
2. Add the coconut flour in the first bowl.
3. In the second bowl, beat the egg and stir in the cream.
4. Mix the pork rind and Parmesan cheese in the third bowl.
5. Dip the onion rings in the first, second and third bowls.
6. Repeat the steps to coat the onion rings twice.
7. Put on a baking pan.
8. Bake in the oven at 425 degrees F for 15 minutes.

Nutritional Value:

- Calories 295
- Total Fat 18.8g
- Saturated Fat 8.1g
- Cholesterol 219mg
- Sodium 678mg
- Total Carbohydrate 5.9g
- Dietary Fiber 1.2g
- Total Sugars 2.7g
- Protein 26.8g
- Potassium 145mg

Cheesy Jalapeno Bites

Preparation Time: 10 minutes
Cooking Time: 20 minutes
Servings: 6

Ingredients:

- 1 ½ cups almond flour
- 1 ½ teaspoons baking powder
- Salt and pepper to taste
- 3 tablespoons butter, cubed
- 1 egg, beaten
- ¼ cup heavy cream
- ½ cup cheddar cheese, shredded
- ¼ cup jalapeno pepper, diced
- 2 teaspoons dried parsley

Method:

1. Preheat your oven to 350 degrees F.
2. Combine the dry ingredients in a bowl.
3. Stir in the butter to this mixture.
4. Stir in the egg and cream.
5. Add the rest of the ingredients.
6. Mix well.
7. Form balls from the mixture and add to a cookie pan.
8. Bake for 20 minutes.

Nutritional Value:

- Calories 280
- Total Fat 26.2 g
- Saturated Fat 12 g
- Cholesterol 200 mg
- Sodium 52 mg
- Total Carbohydrate 6 g
- Dietary Fiber 3 g
- Protein 8.5 g
- Total Sugars 1 g
- Potassium 247 mg

Popcorn Chicken

Preparation Time: 20 minutes
Cooking Time: 25 minutes
Servings: 3

Ingredients:

- ½ lb. chicken, sliced into bite size pieces
- Salt and pepper to taste
- 1 egg, beaten
- 1 tablespoon heavy whipping cream
- ¾ cup almond flour
- ½ teaspoon onion powder
- ½ teaspoon garlic powder
- 2 teaspoons dried oregano

Method:

1. Dry chicken with paper towel.
2. Season with salt and pepper.
3. In a bowl, mix the egg and cream.
4. In another bowl, combine the flour, onion powder, garlic powder and oregano.
5. Dip the chicken into the egg mixture and then coat with flour.
6. Place on a baking tray.
7. Bake in the oven at 400 degrees F for 20 minutes.

Nutritional Value:

- Calories 285
- Total Fat 14.7 g
- Saturated Fat 7 g
- Cholesterol 210 mg
- Sodium 110 mg
- Total Carbohydrate 6 g
- Dietary Fiber 3 g
- Protein 29.3 g
- Total Sugars 1 g
- Potassium 450 mg

Deviled Eggs

Preparation Time: 30 minutes
Cooking Time: 10 minutes
Servings: 6

Ingredients:

- 6 hard boiled eggs, peeled and sliced in half
- ½ teaspoon mustard
- 3 tablespoons mayonnaise
- Salt and pepper to taste
- 4 teaspoons chives
- 4 teaspoons bacon, chopped

Method:

1. Scoop out the yolks from the eggs.
2. Mash in a bowl.
3. Stir in the mustard and mayo.
4. Season with salt and pepper.
5. Mix well.
6. Scoop the yolk mixture on top of each egg white.
7. Sprinkle chives and bacon on top.

Nutritional Value:

- Calories 131.6
- Total Fat 10.75 g
- Saturated Fat 8 g
- Cholesterol 212 mg
- Sodium 115 mg
- Total Carbohydrate 0.4 g
- Dietary Fiber 1 g
- Protein 6.25 g
- Total Sugars 0 g
- Potassium 121 mg

Bacon & Jalapeno Poppers

Preparation Time: 5 minutes
Cooking Time: 40 minutes
Servings: 16

Ingredients:

- 6 oz. ground beef
- Salt and pepper to taste
- 2 oz. cream cheese
- 8 medium jalapenos, sliced in half and seeded
- 8 slices bacon

Method:

1. Add the ground beef to a pan over medium heat.
2. Season with salt and pepper.
3. Cook for 5 to 7 minutes, stirring occasionally.
4. Remove from heat and drain.
5. Add cream cheese to the jalapeno.
6. Top with the ground beef.
7. Wrap each one with bacon.
8. Bake in the oven at 400 degrees F for 30 minutes.

Nutritional Value:

- Calories 56.9
- Total Fat 8.6 g
- Saturated Fat 5 g
- Cholesterol 119 mg
- Sodium 232 mg
- Total Carbohydrate 0.8 g
- Dietary Fiber 0.2 g
- Protein 3.5 g
- Total Sugars 0 g
- Potassium 175 mg

Mushroom Poppers

Preparation Time: 15 minutes
Cooking Time: 30 minutes
Servings: 20

Ingredients:

- 20 big mushroom buttons
- 1 teaspoon olive oil
- 2 sausage links
- 1 onion, chopped
- ½ teaspoon garlic, minced
- Salt and pepper to taste
- 1 cup cheddar cheese, shredded

Method:

1. Remove the stalks of the mushroom and sliced into bits.
2. Remove the sausage from the casing and crumble.
3. In a pan over medium heat, add the olive oil and cook the onion, garlic and sausage for 5 to 10 minutes.
4. Season with salt and pepper.
5. Remove from heat and drain.
6. Mix the mushroom bits with the onion mixture.
7. Put the mushroom mixture into the mushroom caps.
8. Top with the cheese.
9. Place mushroom caps on a baking pan.
10. Bake in the oven at 350 degrees F for 20 minutes.

Nutritional Value:

- Calories 130
- Total Fat 16.4g
- Saturated Fat 8.4g
- Cholesterol 17mg
- Sodium 159mg
- Total Carbohydrate 9.1g
- Dietary Fiber 2.8g
- Total Sugars 0.7g
- Protein 11.7g
- Potassium 54mg

Tortillas

Preparation Time: 5 minutes
Cooking Time: 15 minutes
Servings: 16

Ingredients:

- 10 tablespoons water
- 1/3 cup coconut flour
- ¼ teaspoon baking powder
- 8 egg whites
- Salt to taste
- ¼ teaspoon garlic powder
- ¼ teaspoon onion powder
- ¼ teaspoon chili powder
- 2 tablespoons olive oil

Method:

1. In a bowl, mix the water, flour, baking powder and egg whites.
2. Stir in the rest of the ingredients.
3. Pour the oil into the pan.
4. Place on a medium heat.
5. When it's hot enough, pour the batter into the pan.
6. Spread it thinly.
7. Cook until the surface starts to bubble.
8. Flip and cook another minute.
9. Stuff your tortilla with your preferred keto-friendly toppings.

Nutritional Value:

- Calories 48
- Total Fat 8g
- Saturated Fat 0g
- Cholesterol 0mg
- Sodium 143mg
- Total Carbohydrate 1.3g
- Dietary Fiber 0.1g
- Protein 9.7g
- Total Sugars 0.8g
- Potassium 195mg

Crunchy Goat Cheese

Preparation Time: 10 minutes
Cooking Time: 5 minutes
Servings: 8

Ingredients:

- 1 ½ cups coconut oil
- 8 oz. goat cheese, sliced into strips
- ½ cup coconut flour
- 2 eggs, beaten
- 1 oz. pork rinds, finely ground
- ½ teaspoon dried parsley

Method:

1. Pour the coconut oil into a pan over medium high heat.
2. Put the flour in a bowl.
3. In another bowl, add the eggs.
4. In the third bowl, mix the pork rinds and parsley.
5. Dip the goat cheese in the first, second and third bowls.
6. Add to the hot oil and cook for 30 seconds.
7. Flip and cook for another 30 seconds.
8. Do the same for the rest of the goat strips.
9. Drain on a plate lined with paper towel.

Nutritional Value:

- Calories 517
- Total Fat 53.3g
- Saturated Fat 43.2g
- Cholesterol 76mg
- Sodium 182mg
- Total Carbohydrate 0.7g
- Dietary Fiber 0g
- Protein 12.3g
- Total Sugars 0.7g
- Potassium 29mg

Crispy Parmesan Bites

Preparation Time: 10 minutes
Cooking Time: 10 minutes
Servings: 2

Ingredients:

- 8 tablespoons Parmesan cheese, grated
- 2 slices Provolone cheese, sliced into small bits
- 1 jalapeno, fried and minced

Method:

1. Scoop out Parmesan cheese on top of a baking pan, placing them one inch apart from each other.
2. Top each mound with Provolone and jalapeno bits.
3. Bake in the oven at 425 degrees F for 10 minutes.

Nutritional Value:

- Calories 280
- Total Fat 19.5g
- Saturated Fat 12.8g
- Cholesterol 59mg
- Sodium 765mg
- Total Carbohydrate 3g
- Dietary Fiber 0.2g
- Total Sugars 0.4g
- Protein 25.3g
- Potassium 54mg

Chapter 8: Beef, Pork & Lamb

Beef Egg Roll Slaw

Preparation Time: 15 minutes
Cooking Time: 15 minutes
Servings: 6

Ingredients:

- 2 tablespoons sesame oil
- ½ cup onion, diced
- 3 cloves garlic, crushed and minced
- 5 green onions, chopped
- 1 ½ lb. ground beef
- 1 tablespoon chili garlic sauce
- ½ teaspoon ground ginger
- Salt and pepper to taste
- 3 tablespoons soy sauce
- 14 oz. coleslaw mix
- 1 tablespoon apple cider vinegar

Method:

1. Pour the oil into a pan over medium heat.
2. Cook the onion, garlic and green onion for 5 minutes.
3. Stir in the ground beef, ginger and chili garlic sauce.
4. Season with salt and pepper.
5. Cook for 5 minutes, stirring frequently.
6. Add the rest of the ingredients.
7. Cook for 4 more minutes.

Nutritional Value:

- Calories: 350
- Total Fat 24g
- Saturated Fat 8.0g
- Cholesterol 75mg
- Sodium 694mg
- Total Carbohydrates 12g
- Dietary Fiber 1.8g
- Protein 20.6g
- Total Sugars 1g
- Potassium 439mg

Bacon Cheeseburger Casserole

Preparation Time: 15 minutes
Cooking Time: 35 minutes
Servings: 12

Ingredients:

- 1 teaspoon olive oil
- 2 cloves garlic, crushed and minced
- 2 lb. ground beef
- ½ teaspoon onion powder
- 1 lb. bacon, chopped
- 8 eggs, beaten
- 1 cup heavy whipping cream
- Salt and pepper to taste
- 12 oz. cheddar cheese, shredded

Method:

1. Preheat your oven to 350 degrees F.
2. Pour the oil into a pan over medium heat.
3. Cook the garlic for 30 seconds.
4. Add the beef and season with onion powder.
5. Cook for 5 minutes.
6. Drain the beef.
7. Spread on a casserole pan.
8. Sprinkle the bacon bits on top.
9. In a bowl, mix the eggs with the rest of the ingredients.
10. Pour the egg mixture on top of the beef.
11. Bake in the oven for 30 minutes.

Nutritional Value:

- Calories 457
- Total Fat 36.9g
- Saturated Fat 18.0g
- Cholesterol 241mg
- Sodium 656mg
- Total Carbohydrates 1.6g
- Dietary Fiber 0g
- Protein 28.7g
- Total Sugars 0g
- Potassium 317mg

Korean Beef

Preparation Time: 10 minutes
Cooking Time: 10 minutes
Servings: 4

Ingredients:

- 2 teaspoons sesame oil
- 3 cloves garlic, crushed and minced
- 1 lb. ground beef
- ¼ teaspoon ground ginger
- 1 tablespoon coconut sugar
- ¼ cup soy sauce
- Pepper to taste
- 2 cups cauliflower rice
- 1 tablespoon sesame seeds
- 2 tablespoons green onions, chopped

Method:

1. Pour the oil into a pan over medium heat.
2. Cook the garlic and ground beef for 7 minutes.
3. In a bowl, mix the ginger, sugar, soy sauce and pepper.
4. Pour the mixture into the pan and mix.
5. Simmer for 3 minutes.
6. Serve on top of cauliflower rice.
7. Garnish with the sesame seeds and green onions before serving.

Nutritional Value:

- Calories 297
- Total Fat 19.1g
- Saturated Fat 7.0g
- Cholesterol 68mg
- Sodium 982mg
- Total Carbohydrates 8.9g
- Dietary Fiber 1.8g
- Protein 22.4g
- Total Sugars 5g
- Potassium 465mg

Beef Tagliata

Preparation Time: 20 minutes
Cooking Time: 20 minutes
Servings: 6

Ingredients:

- 1 teaspoon fresh oregano, chopped
- 2 teaspoons fresh rosemary, chopped
- 3 cloves garlic, crushed and minced
- Salt and pepper to taste
- 2 lb. sirloin steaks
- 1 tablespoon olive oil
- 6 cups arugula
- 2 teaspoons olive oil
- 1 teaspoon freshly squeezed lemon juice
- ¼ lemon, sliced
- 2 oz. Parmesan cheese, grated

Method:

1. Put your cast-iron pan inside the oven to preheat.
2. Mix the oregano, rosemary, garlic, salt and pepper in a bowl.
3. Season the steak with this mixture.
4. Pour the oil into the preheated pan and place over medium heat.
5. Cook for 10 minutes per side.
6. Let sit for 10 minutes before slicing.
7. Arrange the arugula on a serving plate.
8. Top with the steak slices.
9. Drizzle with the mixture of lemon juice and olive oil.
10. Sprinkle the Parmesan cheese on top.

Nutritional Value:

- Calories 333
- Total Fat 14.5g
- Saturated Fat 5.0g
- Cholesterol 86mg
- Sodium 1117mg
- Total Carbohydrates 3g
- Dietary Fiber 0.8g
- Protein 45.5g
- Total Sugars 1g
- Potassium 650mg

Pork Belly Cracklings

Preparation Time: 1 hour and 20 minutes
Cooking Time: 40 minutes
Servings: 12

Ingredients:

- 3 lb. pork belly
- Water
- 3 tablespoons Cajun seasoning powder, divided

Method:

1. Freeze the pork belly for 45 minutes.
2. Slice into cubes.
3. Fill your pot with water.
4. Add 1 teaspoon Cajun seasoning.
5. Place the pork cubes into the pot.
6. Cook until the water has evaporated.
7. Cook the pork in its own oil for about 15 minutes or until crispy.
8. Season with the remaining Cajun powder.

Nutritional Value:

- Calories 209
- Total Fat 15.8g
- Saturated Fat 5.0g
- Cholesterol 41mg
- Sodium 1340mg
- Potassium 241mg
- Total Carbohydrates 1.7g
- Dietary Fiber 0.2g
- Protein 14.1g
- Sugars 0g

Bacon Salad

Preparation Time: 10 minutes
Cooking Time: 5 minutes
Servings: 4

Ingredients:

- 4 oz. arugula
- 8 oz. thick bacon slices
- ½ cup cherry tomatoes, sliced in half
- 1 tablespoon olive oil
- 1 tablespoon balsamic vinegar
- Salt and pepper to taste
- 1/8 cup Parmesan cheese, shaved

Method:

1. Preheat your grill.
2. Grill the bacon for 2 minutes.
3. Flip and grill for another 1 minute.
4. Arrange the arugula on a serving plate.
5. Top with the bacon and tomatoes.
6. In a small bowl, mix the oil, vinegar, salt and pepper.
7. Drizzle the salad with this mixture.
8. Sprinkle the shaved Parmesan cheese on top.

Nutritional Value:

- Calories 155
- Total Fat 12.1g
- Saturated Fat 3.0g
- Cholesterol 23mg
- Sodium 556mg
- Total Carbohydrates 3g
- Dietary Fiber 0.7g
- Protein 8.7g
- Total Sugars 1g
- Potassium 259mg

Tuscan Pork

Preparation Time: 5 minutes
Cooking Time: 25 minutes
Servings: 12

Ingredients:

- 2 teaspoons dried oregano
- 2 teaspoons dried rosemary
- 4 teaspoons garlic, crushed and minced
- Salt and pepper to taste
- 4 lb. pork tenderloin

Method:

1. Preheat your oven to 425 degrees F.
2. In a bowl, mix all the ingredients except the pork.
3. Rub all sides of the pork with the mixture.
4. Put the pork on a baking pan and bake for 25 minutes.
5. Let sit for 5 minutes before slicing and serving.

Nutritional Value:

- Calories 183
- Total Fat 7.3g
- Saturated Fat 3g
- Cholesterol 84mg
- Sodium 251mg
- Total Carbohydrates 0.7g
- Dietary Fiber 0.3g
- Protein 26.9g
- Total Sugars 0g
- Potassium 410mg

Baked Bacon

Preparation Time: 5 minutes
Cooking Time: 30 minutes
Servings: 6

Ingredients:

- 16 oz. bacon

Method:

1. Preheat your oven to 350 degrees F.
2. Cover your baking pan with parchment paper.
3. Arrange the bacon slices on the baking pan.
4. Bake in the oven for 15 minutes.
5. Flip and bake for another 15 minutes or until crispy.

Nutritional Value:

- Calories 134
- Total Fat 10.4g
- Saturated Fat 3.0g
- Cholesterol 27mg
- Sodium 574mg
- Potassium 140mg
- Total Carbohydrates 0.4g
- Dietary Fiber 0g
- Protein 9.2g
- Sugars 0g

Lamb Chops with Herb Butter

Preparation Time: 5 minutes
Cooking Time: 30 minutes
Servings: 4

Ingredients:

- 8 lamb chops
- Salt and pepper
- 1 tablespoon butter
- 1 tablespoon olive oil
- 4 oz. herb butter
- 1 lemon, sliced in wedges

Method:

1. Season the lamb chops with salt and pepper.
2. In a pan over medium heat, add the butter and olive oil.
3. Cook the lamb chops until brown and fully cooked on the inside.
4. Serve with the herb butter and garnish with the lemon wedges.

Nutritional Value:

- Calories 636
- Total Fat 27.2g
- Saturated Fat 9.7g
- Cholesterol 298mg
- Sodium 259mg
- Total Carbohydrate 0g
- Dietary Fiber 0g
- Total Sugars 0g
- Protein 91.8g
- Potassium 1096mg

Slow Cooked Lamb Shanks

Preparation Time: 15 minutes
Cooking Time: 8 hours and 10 minutes
Servings: 6

Ingredients:

- 1 tablespoon olive oil
- 6 lamb shanks
- Salt and pepper to taste
- 1 onion, chopped
- 2 stalks celery, chopped
- 2 carrots, chopped
- 1 tablespoon dried oregano
- 1 cup red wine
- 1 ½ cups chicken stock
- 1 ½ tablespoons fresh rosemary
- 1 can crushed tomatoes
- 3 bay leaves

Method:

1. Add the olive oil to a pan over medium heat.
2. Cook the lamb shanks on both sides.
3. Season with salt and pepper.
4. Set aside.
5. Add the onion, celery and carrots.
6. Cook for 5 minutes.
7. Transfer the lamb and veggies to a slow cooker.
8. Deglaze the pan with the red wine and simmer for 3 minutes.
9. Transfer to the slow cooker.
10. Stir in the rest of the ingredients.
11. Cook on low for 8 hours.

Nutritional Value:

- Calories 465
- Total Fat 23 g
- Saturated Fat 10 g
- Cholesterol 162 mg

- Sodium 980 mg
- Total Carbohydrate 9 g
- Dietary Fiber 1 g
- Protein 43 g
- Total Sugars 2 g
- Potassium 769 mg

Greek Meatballs

Preparation Time: 10 minutes
Cooking Time: 10 minutes
Servings: 4

Ingredients:

- 6 cups ground lamb
- 1 egg, beaten
- Salt and pepper to taste
- 1 teaspoon garlic paste
- ¼ cup almond flour
- ½ teaspoon cumin
- 1 ½ tablespoons oregano
- ½ teaspoon mint
- ½ teaspoon coriander
- 2 tablespoons olive oil

Method:

1. Combine all the ingredients except the olive oil.
2. Form balls from the mixture.
3. Pour the olive oil into a pan over medium heat.
4. Cook the meatballs until brown on all sides.

Nutritional Value:

- Calories 513
- Total Fat 43 g
- Saturated Fat 15 g
- Cholesterol 99 mg
- Sodium 246 mg
- Total Carbohydrate 7 g
- Dietary Fiber 1 g
- Protein 23 g
- Total Sugars 1 g
- Potassium 319 mg

Garlic & Rosemary Lamb

Preparation Time: 20 minutes
Cooking Time: 25 minutes
Servings: 3

Ingredients:

- 2 cloves garlic, crushed and minced
- 3 tablespoons fresh rosemary, chopped
- 4 tablespoons ghee
- Salt and pepper to taste
- 6 lamb chops

Method:

1. Mix all the ingredients except the lamb chops.
2. Wrap the ghee with plastic sheet and refrigerate until firm.
3. Season the lamb chops with salt and pepper.
4. Bake in the oven for 20 minutes.
5. Unwrap the ghee and put on top of the lamb chops.
6. Bake for another 5 minutes.

Nutritional Value:

- Calories 517
- Total Fat 24.5g
- Saturated Fat 10.5g
- Cholesterol 237mg
- Sodium 187mg
- Total Carbohydrate 1.1g
- Dietary Fiber 0.6g
- Protein 69g
- Total Sugars 0g
- Potassium 837mg

Chapter 9: Poultry

Baked Cajun Chicken

Preparation Time: 10 minutes
Cooking Time: 30 minutes
Servings: 8

Ingredients:

- 8 chicken drumsticks
- 2 tablespoons vegetable oil
- Salt and pepper to taste
- 1 teaspoon paprika
- ¼ teaspoon cayenne pepper
- ½ teaspoon garlic powder
- ½ teaspoon onion powder
- ¼ teaspoon dried thyme
- ½ teaspoon dried basil
- ½ teaspoon dried oregano

Method:

1. Preheat your oven to 400 degrees F.
2. Cover your baking sheet with parchment paper.
3. Add the chicken to a bowl.
4. Coat with oil.
5. Season with the mixture of all the herbs and spices.
6. Coat evenly.
7. Bake in the oven for 25 minutes.
8. Transfer to a broiler and broil for 5 minutes.

Nutritional Value:

- Calories 170
- Total Fat 9.2g
- Saturated Fat 2.0g
- Cholesterol 66mg
- Sodium 213mg
- Total Carbohydrates 0.6g
- Dietary Fiber 0.3g
- Protein 20.2g
- Total Sugars 0g
- Potassium 192mg

Chicken in Creamy Lemon Garlic Sauce

Preparation Time: 10 minutes
Cooking Time: 40 minutes
Servings: 4

Ingredients:

- 2 tablespoons olive oil
- 4 chicken thighs
- Salt and pepper to taste
- 1 onion, sliced thinly
- 4 cloves garlic, crushed and minced
- ½ cup dry white wine
- 3 tablespoons lemon juice
- 1 cup chicken broth
- 2 tablespoons butter
- ½ cup heavy cream
- ½ teaspoon thyme leaves

Method:

1. Season the chicken with salt and pepper.
2. Pour the oil into a pan over medium heat.
3. Cook the chicken for 3 minutes per side.
4. Set aside.
5. Add the onion and cook for 1 minute.
6. Add the garlic and cook for 30 seconds.
7. Deglaze the pan with the wine.
8. Stir in lemon juice and broth.
9. Add the chicken and onion mixture with sauce into a pressure cooker.
10. Seal the pot.
11. Cook on high for 15 minutes.
12. Release the pressure naturally.
13. Put the chicken back to the pan with the cooking liquid.
14. Stir in the rest of the ingredients.
15. Cook until the sauce has thickened.
16. Pour sauce over the chicken before serving.

Nutritional Value:

- Calories 445
- Total Fat 35.6g
- Saturated Fat 15.0g
- Cholesterol 128mg
- Sodium 521mg

- Total Carbohydrates 5.2g
- Dietary Fiber 0.4g
- Protein 20.5g
- Total Sugars 2g
- Potassium 262mg

Spicy Chicken Fritters

Preparation Time: 20 minutes
Cooking Time: 10 minutes
Servings: 12

Ingredients:

- 2 eggs, beaten
- 1 lb. ground chicken
- ½ cup onion, chopped
- 3 cloves garlic, minced
- 4 oz. green chili, chopped
- 2 tablespoons mayonnaise
- ½ cup almond flour
- ½ teaspoon ground cumin
- 1 teaspoon chipotle chili powder
- 2 teaspoons chili powder
- Salt and pepper to taste
- 2 tablespoons Buffalo sauce
- ¼ cup avocado oil

Method:

1. Mix all the ingredients except oil in a bowl.
2. Form patties from the mixture.
3. In a pan over medium heat, add the oil.
4. Cook the chicken fritters for 3 minutes per side.
5. Cook in batches.

Nutritional Value:

- Calories 164
- Total Fat 12.6g
- Saturated Fat 2.0g
- Cholesterol 58mg
- Sodium 426mg
- Total Carbohydrates 3.6g
- Dietary Fiber 1g
- Protein 9.7g
- Total Sugars 1g
- Potassium 118mg

Spicy Chicken Wings with Mustard

Preparation Time: 10 minutes
Cooking Time: 10 minutes
Servings: 20

Ingredients:

- Cooking spray
- 1 tablespoon soy sauce
- ¼ cup butter
- ¼ cup sweetener
- 2 tablespoons Dijon mustard
- 1/3 cup hot sauce
- ¼ teaspoon salt
- ¼ teaspoon onion powder
- ¼ teaspoon ground ginger
- 5 lb. chicken wings, cooked

Method:

1. Preheat your oven to 400 degrees F.
2. Spray your baking pan with oil.
3. Combine all the ingredients except chicken in a bowl.
4. Mix well.
5. Add to a pan over medium low heat and cook for 5 minutes.
6. Remove from heat.
7. Toss the chicken in the sauce.
8. Arrange the chicken on a baking pan.
9. Bake for 10 minutes.

Nutritional Value:

- Calories 354
- Total Fat 24.4g
- Saturated Fat 8.0g
- Cholesterol 101mg
- Sodium 390mg
- Total Carbohydrates 0.9g
- Dietary Fiber 0.1g
- Protein 30.6g
- Total Sugars 0g
- Potassium 212mg

Baked Paprika Chicken

Preparation Time: 5 minutes
Cooking Time: 35 minutes
Servings: 2

Ingredients:

- Salt and pepper to taste
- 1 teaspoon smoked paprika
- 1 teaspoon garlic powder
- ½ teaspoon parsley flakes
- ½ teaspoon ground mustard
- 1 tablespoon olive oil
- 2 tablespoons butter
- 2 chicken breast fillets

Method:

1. Preheat your oven to 400 degrees F.
2. Combine all the ingredients except the oil, butter and chicken.
3. Mix well.
4. Coat the chicken with oil.
5. Put on a baking pan.
6. Sprinkle both sides with the spice mixture.
7. Top each chicken with butter.
8. Bake in the oven for 35 minutes.

Nutritional Value:

- Calories 552
- Total Fat 26.9g
- Saturated Fat 11.0g
- Cholesterol 224mg
- Sodium 834mg
- Total Carbohydrates 2.3g
- Dietary Fiber 0.8g
- Protein 71.6g
- Total Sugars 0g
- Potassium 636mg

Grilled Lemon Chicken

Preparation Time: 1 hour and 10 minutes
Cooking Time: 20 minutes
Servings: 4

Ingredients:

- 1 tablespoon lemon juice
- 1 teaspoon lemon zest
- ¼ cup olive oil
- 1 tablespoon garlic paste
- 3 sprigs fresh parsley
- Salt to taste
- 8 chicken thighs

Method:

1. Combine all the ingredients except the chicken in a sealable bag.
2. Shake to combine well.
3. Add the chicken to the bag and seal.
4. Marinate in the refrigerator for 1 hour.
5. Remove from the bag and grill for 8 to 10 minutes per side.
6. Garnish with lemon wedges.

Nutritional Value:

- Calories 511
- Total Fat 37.4g
- Saturated Fat 9.0g
- Cholesterol 142mg
- Sodium 432mg
- Total Carbohydrates 4.6g
- Dietary Fiber 2g
- Protein 39.3g
- Total Sugars 0g
- Potassium 499mg

Chicken Strips

Preparation Time: 10 minutes
Cooking Time: 20 minutes
Servings: 15

Ingredients:

- ½ cup Parmesan cheese, grated
- 1 cup pork rinds, crushed
- Salt to taste
- 2 teaspoons Italian seasoning
- 1 teaspoon dried basil
- 1 teaspoon dried thyme
- ½ cup melted butter
- 3 chicken breasts fillets, sliced into strips

Method:

1. Preheat your oven to 400 degrees F.
2. Cover your baking pan with parchment paper.
3. Combine all the ingredients except the butter and chicken breast in a bowl.
4. Dip the chicken strips in butter and then with the pork rind mixture.
5. Put on the baking pan.
6. Bake in the oven for 20 minutes.

Nutritional Value:

- Calories 178
- Total Fat 14g
- Saturated Fat 7.0g
- Cholesterol 53mg
- Sodium 321mg
- Total Carbohydrates 0.4g
- Dietary Fiber 0.2g
- Protein 14.5g
- Total Sugars 0g
- Potassium 52mg

Garlic Chicken

Preparation Time: 10 minutes
Cooking Time: 25 minutes
Servings: 6

Ingredients:

- 6 chicken breast fillet
- Salt and pepper to taste
- ½ teaspoon smoked paprika
- 1 teaspoon garlic powder
- 3 tablespoons butter
- 2 onions, sliced
- 3 cloves garlic, crushed and minced
- 1 cup chicken broth

Method:

1. Season both sides of chicken with salt, pepper, paprika and garlic powder.
2. Add butter to a pan over medium heat.
3. Cook the chicken for 3 minutes per side.
4. Stir in the onions and garlic and cook for 5 more minutes.
5. Transfer the chicken, onions and garlic to a pressure cooker.
6. Pour in the broth.
7. Cook on high for 15 minutes.

Nutritional Value:

- Calories 230
- Total Fat 8.7g
- Saturated Fat 4.0g
- Cholesterol 81mg
- Sodium 327mg
- Total Carbohydrates 12g
- Dietary Fiber 2.3g
- Protein 25.3g
- Total Sugars 5g
- Potassium 406mg

Barbecue Chicken

Preparation Time: 10 minutes
Cooking Time: 15 minutes
Servings: 3

Ingredients:

- Cooking spray
- 6 chicken thigh fillets
- Salt and pepper to taste
- 1 cup barbecue sauce, divided

Method:

1. Preheat your grill. Grease the grate with cooking spray.
2. Sprinkle both sides of chicken with salt and pepper.
3. Brush chicken with barbecue sauce before placing on the grill.
4. Grill for 3 minutes per side, brushing with the sauce frequently.

Nutritional Value:

- Calories 308
- Total Fat 13.8g
- Saturated Fat 4.0g
- Cholesterol 78mg
- Sodium 817mg
- Total Carbohydrates 12.7g
- Dietary Fiber 0.4g
- Protein 21.5g
- Total Sugars 16g
- Potassium 287mg

Chicken Curry

Preparation Time: 10 minutes
Cooking Time: 25 minutes
Servings: 4

Ingredients:

- 3 tablespoons butter
- 1 tablespoon tomato paste
- 1 tablespoon red curry paste
- ½ cup onion, chopped
- 2 cloves garlic, crushed and minced
- 2 chicken breast fillets, sliced into smaller portions
- ¼ cup heavy whipping cream
- ½ cup coconut milk
- 1 teaspoon yellow curry powder
- ½ teaspoon garam masala
- ½ teaspoon ground turmeric
- ½ teaspoon sweetener

Method:

1. Add the butter to a pan over medium heat.
2. Stir in the red curry paste and tomato paste.
3. Cook for 3 minutes.
4. Add the onion, garlic and chicken.
5. Cook for 5 minutes.
6. Transfer to your pressure cooker.
7. Pour in the cream and coconut milk to the pot.
8. Seal the pot.
9. Cook on high pressure for 7 minutes.
10. Release pressure quickly.
11. Uncover the pot carefully.
12. Add the rest of the ingredients and mix well.
13. Serve warm.

Nutritional Value:

- Calories 306
- Total Fat 26.9g
- Saturated Fat 17.0g
- Cholesterol 92mg
- Sodium 152mg

- Total Carbohydrates 5.8g
- Dietary Fiber 1.2g
- Protein 17.6g
- Sugars 1g
- Potassium 292mg

Chapter 10: Seafood

Herbed Salmon

Preparation Time: 10 minutes
Cooking Time: 8 minutes
Servings: 4

Ingredients:

- 4 salmon fillets
- Salt and pepper to taste
- 2 sprigs fresh rosemary, chopped
- 1 teaspoon dried basil, crushed
- 1 tablespoon olive oil
- 1 tablespoon butter

Method:

1. Season both sides of salmon with salt and pepper.
2. Sprinkle both sides with rosemary and basil.
3. Add oil and butter to a pan over medium heat.
4. Cook the salmon for 3 minutes per side.

Nutritional Value:

- Calories 245
- Total Fat 24.6g
- Saturated Fat 8.0g
- Cholesterol 166mg
- Sodium 147mg
- Total Carbohydrates 4.2g
- Dietary Fiber 0.2g
- Protein 36g
- Total Sugars 1g
- Potassium 491mg

Crab Salad

Preparation Time: 40 minutes
Cooking Time: 0 minutes
Servings: 2

Ingredients:

- 8 oz. crab meat, chopped
- ½ cup celery, diced
- ¼ cup green bell pepper, diced
- 1/8 cup scallions, diced
- 3 tablespoons mayonnaise
- 1 tablespoon freshly squeezed lemon juice
- 1 teaspoon adobo seasoning
- Salt and pepper to taste
- 4 cups Romaine lettuce, torn

Method:

1. In a bowl, combine all the ingredients except the lettuce.
2. Mix well.
3. Cover the bowl with foil.
4. Put in the refrigerator for 30 minutes.
5. Serve with the Romaine lettuce.

Nutritional Value:

- Calories 265
- Total Fat 17.1g
- Saturated Fat 3.0g
- Cholesterol 30mg
- Sodium 1139mg
- Total Carbohydrates 19.6g
- Dietary Fiber 1.4g
- Protein 9.1g
- Total Sugars 8g
- Potassium 172mg

Lemon & Butter Shrimp

Preparation Time: 10 minutes
Cooking Time: 30 minutes
Servings: 4

Ingredients:

- 1 teaspoon olive oil
- 1 lb. shrimp, peeled and deveined
- ½ teaspoon Creole seasoning
- 1 tablespoon butter
- 3 sprigs thyme
- 4 teaspoons lemon zest, divided

Method:

1. Sprinkle shrimp with Creole seasoning.
2. Add olive oil to a pan over medium heat.
3. Add the shrimp to the pan and cook for 2 minutes, stirring frequently.
4. Stir in butter, thyme and half of lemon zest.
5. Cook while stirring for 3 more minutes.
6. Garnish with remaining lemon zest.
7. Discard the thyme sprigs before serving.

Nutritional Value:

- Calories 212
- Total Fat 15.7g
- Saturated Fat 9.0g
- Cholesterol 203mg
- Sodium 340mg
- Total Carbohydrates 6g
- Dietary Fiber 3.4g
- Protein 19.9g
- Total Sugars 0g
- Potassium 304mg

Salmon Patties

Preparation Time: 15 minutes
Cooking Time: 20 minutes
Servings: 4

Ingredients:

- 3 teaspoons olive oil
- 14 oz. canned salmon, drained and crushed into flakes
- 1 red bell pepper, chopped
- ¼ cup fresh parsley, chopped
- 2 tablespoons Dijon mustard
- 2 tablespoons capers, chopped
- Salt and pepper to taste
- ½ cup almond meal

Method:

1. Preheat your oven to 450 degrees F.
2. Grease your baking pan with a little oil.
3. Place inside the oven.
4. Combine all the ingredients in a large bowl.
5. Form patties from this mixture.
6. Add to the baking pan.
7. Drizzle the top with the remaining oil.
8. Bake for 20 minutes.

Nutritional Value:

- Calories 226
- Total Fat 9.8g
- Saturated Fat 1.0g
- Cholesterol 70mg
- Sodium 742mg
- Potassium 252mg
- Total Carbohydrates 7g
- Dietary Fiber 0.6g
- Protein 30.4g
- Sugars 1g

Coconut Shrimp

Preparation Time: 20 minutes
Cooking Time: 5 minutes
Servings: 4

Ingredients:

- ¼ cup coconut flour
- ½ teaspoon garlic powder
- ½ teaspoon onion powder
- 2 eggs
- 1 cup macadamia nuts
- 1 cup shredded coconut (unsweetened)
- 1 lb. shrimp, peeled and deveined
- 2 tablespoons ghee
- Salt and pepper to taste

Method:

1. In a bowl, combine the flour, garlic powder and onion powder.
2. In another bowl, beat the eggs.
3. Add the nuts to the food processor and pulse until chopped.
4. Put the nuts in a third bowl.
5. Stir in the coconut shreds.
6. Dip the shrimp in the first, second and third bowls.
7. Pour the ghee into a pan over medium heat.
8. Cook the shrimp for 2 minutes per side.
9. Season with salt and pepper.

Nutritional Value:

- Calories 732
- Total Fat 60.7g
- Saturated Fat 24.0g
- Cholesterol 255mg
- Sodium 426mg
- Total Carbohydrates 26.6g
- Dietary Fiber 10.5g
- Protein 27.2g
- Total Sugars 4g
- Potassium 485mg

Clam Chowder

Preparation Time: 20 minutes
Cooking Time: 30 minutes
Servings: 2

Ingredients:

- 2 tablespoons butter
- ¼ cup celery, chopped
- ¼ cup red bell pepper, chopped
- 3 cups chicken stock
- 6 shrimp, peeled and deveined
- 8 oz. canned baby clams
- 6 slices bacon, fried and crumbled
- 1 cup cauliflower, chopped
- 1 teaspoon seafood chowder spice
- 8 spears asparagus, chopped
- ½ cup cream
- Salt and pepper to taste

Method:

1. Add the butter to a pan over medium heat.
2. Cook the celery and red bell pepper for 5 minutes.
3. Pour in the stock.
4. Bring to a boil.
5. Reduce heat to medium low.
6. Add the shrimp, clams, bacon and cauliflower.
7. Season with the seafood chowder spice.
8. Simmer for 15 minutes.
9. Stir in the asparagus and simmer for another 5 minutes.
10. Remove from heat.
11. Stir in the cream and season with salt and pepper before serving.

Nutritional Value:

- Calories 709
- Total Fat 48.6g
- Saturated Fat 24.0g
- Cholesterol 257mg

- Sodium 2417mg
- Total Carbohydrates 16.3g
- Dietary Fiber 3.2g

- Protein 51.8g
- Total Sugars 4g
- Potassium 1382mg

Salmon in Creamy Tomato Sauce

Preparation Time: 10 minutes
Cooking Time: 15 minutes
Servings: 2

Ingredients:

- 1 tablespoon olive oil
- 2 slices bacon
- 2 salmon fillets
- Salt and pepper to taste
- 1 onion, sliced
- 1 clove garlic, chopped
- 1 tablespoon tomato paste
- ½ cup cream
- 5 tablespoons water
- 10 basil leaves, snipped
- ½ teaspoon lemon zest

Method:

1. Add the olive oil to a pan over medium heat.
2. Cook the bacon until crispy.
3. Transfer to cutting board and chop. Set aside.
4. Season salmon with salt and pepper.
5. Cook in the same pan for 3 minutes per side.
6. Transfer to a plate and set aside.
7. Add onion and garlic to the pan.
8. Stir in the rest of the ingredients.
9. Reduce heat and simmer for 15 minutes.
10. Season the salt with salt and pepper.
11. Pour the sauce over the salmon and sprinkle bacon bits on top before serving.

Nutritional Value:

- Calories 431
- Total Fat 25 g
- Saturated Fat 13 g
- Cholesterol 160 mg
- Sodium 240 mg
- Total Carbohydrate 6 g
- Dietary Fiber 2 g
- Protein 38 g
- Total Sugars 1 g
- Potassium 540 mg

Salmon with Basil & Avocado

Preparation Time: 10 minutes
Cooking Time: 10 minutes
Servings: 4

Ingredients:

- 1 ½ lb. salmon fillets
- 1 teaspoon Italian seasoning
- Salt and pepper to taste
- ½ teaspoon red pepper flakes, crushed
- 2 teaspoons coconut oil
- 1 avocado, sliced and pitted
- 1 tablespoon lime juice
- ¼ cup basil, chopped

Method:

1. Season both sides of the salmon with Italian seasoning, salt, pepper and red pepper flakes.
2. Pour the oil into a pan over medium heat.
3. Cook the salmon for 4 minutes per side.
4. Mash the avocado and stir in the lime juice and basil.
5. Season with salt.
6. Serve salmon with avocado.

Nutritional Value:

- Calories 232
- Total Fat 19 g
- Saturated Fat 9 g
- Cholesterol 104 mg
- Sodium 525 mg
- Total Carbohydrate 7 g
- Dietary Fiber 3 g
- Protein 32 g
- Total Sugars 0 g
- Potassium 862 mg

Baked Cod & Asparagus

Preparation Time: 10 minutes
Cooking Time: 20 minutes
Servings: 4

Ingredients:

- 4 salmon fillets
- Salt and pepper to taste
- 1 lb. asparagus, trimmed
- 2 tablespoons olive oil
- 1 lemon, sliced
- 2 cloves garlic, crushed and minced
- Chopped fresh rosemary

Method:

1. Preheat your oven to 400 degrees F.
2. Season both sides of salmon with salt and pepper.
3. Place on top of a foil sheet.
4. Add the asparagus on top.
5. Drizzle with a little bit of olive oil and season with a little more salt and pepper.
6. Top with the lemon slices, garlic and rosemary.
7. Fold and seal the foil to create a foil pouch.
8. Bake in the oven for 30 minutes.

Nutritional Value:

- Calories 412
- Total Fat 22 g
- Saturated Fat 3 g
- Cholesterol 116 mg
- Sodium 96 mg
- Total Carbohydrate 7 g
- Dietary Fiber 3 g
- Protein 35 g
- Total Sugars 2 g
- Potassium 1308 mg

Trout in Dill Cream Sauce

Preparation Time: 5 minutes
Cooking Time: 15 minutes
Servings: 4

Ingredients:

Sauce

- 2 ½ tablespoons fresh dill, chopped
- 2 teaspoons Dijon mustard
- 2 tablespoons milk
- ¾ cup sour cream
- ½ teaspoon white sugar
- 1 tablespoon lemon juice
- 1 teaspoon lemon zest
- ½ teaspoon garlic powder
- Salt to taste

Fish

- 4 trout fillets
- Salt and pepper to taste
- 1 tablespoon olive oil

Method:

1. Combine all the ingredients for the sauce. Set aside.
2. Season both sides of fish with salt and pepper.
3. Pour the oil in a pan over medium heat.
4. Cook for 2 minutes per side.
5. Serve with the sauce.

Nutritional Value:

- Calories 208
- Total Fat 22.8 g
- Saturated Fat 7.6 g
- Cholesterol 129 mg
- Sodium 305 mg
- Total Carbohydrate 4.2 g
- Dietary Fiber 1 g
- Protein 42 g
- Total Sugars 1.1 g
- Potassium 832 mg

Chapter 11: Soups & Sides

Taco Soup

Preparation Time: 10 minutes
Cooking Time: 20 minutes
Servings: 8

Ingredients:

- 1 tablespoon olive oil
- ½ cup onion, chopped
- 2 cloves garlic, crushed and minced
- 1 lb. ground beef
- 1 teaspoon chili powder
- 1 tablespoon ground cumin
- 30 oz. beef broth
- 8 oz. cream cheese
- ½ cup heavy cream
- 20 oz. canned diced tomatoes
- Salt to taste

Method:

1. Pour the oil into a soup pot.
2. Add the onion, garlic and ground beef.
3. Cook for 5 minutes.
4. Drain the fat.
5. Season with chili powder and cumin.
6. Cook for 2 more minutes.
7. Stir in the rest of the ingredients.
8. Season with salt.
9. Cook for 10 more minutes.

Nutritional Value:

- Calories 288
- Total Fat 24g
- Saturated Fat 13.0g
- Cholesterol 85mg

- Sodium 1310mg
- Total Carbohydrates 5.4g
- Dietary Fiber 1.1g

- Protein 13.4g
- Total Sugars 1g
- Potassium 298mg

Butternut Squash Soup

Preparation Time: 20 minutes
Cooking Time: 35 minutes
Servings: 6

Ingredients:

- 1 tablespoon olive oil
- 1 onion, chopped
- 2 cloves garlic, crushed
- 1 tablespoon brown sugar
- 5 cups vegetable broth
- 1 lb. butternut squash, cubed
- 1 cup heavy whipping cream
- ½ teaspoon ground ginger
- Salt and pepper to taste

Method:

1. Add the oil to a pan over medium heat.
2. Cook onion for 5 minutes.
3. Add the garlic and cook for 1 minute.
4. Add onion and garlic to a pressure cooker.
5. Stir in the rest of the ingredients.
6. Seal the pot.
7. Cook on high pressure for 10 minutes.
8. Release pressure quickly.
9. Transfer to a blender and pulse until smooth and creamy.
10. Reheat before serving the soup.

Nutritional Value:

- Calories 235
- Total Fat 17.5g
- Saturated Fat 9.0g
- Cholesterol 54mg
- Sodium 791mg
- Total Carbohydrates 18.7g
- Dietary Fiber 2.8g
- Protein 2.7g
- Total Sugars 7g
- Potassium 337mg

Cheesy Cauliflower Soup

Preparation Time: 20 minutes
Cooking Time: 35 minutes
Servings: 6

Ingredients:

- 1 tablespoon olive oil
- 1 onion, diced
- 2 cloves garlic, crushed and minced
- 1 head cauliflower, chopped
- Salt and pepper to taste
- 1 tablespoon onion powder
- 32 oz. chicken stock
- 2 cups Cheddar cheese, shredded
- 1 cup half-and-half
- 6 slices turkey bacon, diced
- 1 tablespoon Dijon mustard
- 4 teaspoons hot sauce

Method:

1. Pour the oil into a pan over medium heat.
2. Cook onion and garlic for 3 minutes.
3. Stir in the cauliflower.
4. Season with salt, pepper and onion powder.
5. Cook for 5 minutes, stirring occasionally.
6. Transfer to a pressure cooker.
7. Add the chicken stock.
8. Seal the pot and cook on high for 10 minutes.
9. Release pressure quickly.
10. Uncover the pot.
11. Stir in the rest of the ingredients.
12. Transfer to a soup pot and cook for another 5 minutes.

Nutritional Value:

- Calories 347
- Total Fat 25.6g

- Saturated Fat 13.0g
- Cholesterol 80mg
- Sodium 1181mg
- Total Carbohydrates 13.4g

- Dietary Fiber 3.3g
- Protein 17.7g
- Total Sugars 5g
- Potassium 530mg

Pumpkin & Sausage Soup

Preparation Time: 5 minutes
Cooking Time: 25 minutes
Servings: 6

Ingredients:

- 1 tablespoon butter
- ½ cup onion, chopped
- ½ lb. pork sausage
- 3 cups chicken broth
- 15 oz. canned pumpkin puree
- Salt to taste
- ¼ teaspoon garlic powder
- ¼ cup heavy cream

Method:

1. In a pan over medium heat, add the butter and cook onion and sausage for 5 minutes.
2. Transfer to a soup pot over low heat.
3. Stir in the rest of the rest ingredients except the cream.
4. Simmer for 20 minutes.
5. Stir in the cream before serving.

Nutritional Value:

- Calories 198
- Total Fat 15.4g
- Saturated Fat 7g
- Cholesterol 48mg
- Sodium 1399mg
- Total Carbohydrates 8.4g
- Dietary Fiber 2.3g
- Protein 7g
- Total Sugars 4g
- Potassium 272mg

Cheeseburger Soup

Preparation Time: 15 minutes
Cooking Time: 50 minutes
Servings: 6

Ingredients:

- 1 tablespoon olive oil
- 6 slices bacon
- 1 lb. ground beef
- 3 cups beef broth
- 4 oz. cream cheese
- 1 cup cheddar cheese, shredded
- 1 teaspoon chili powder
- 1 teaspoon onion powder
- Pepper to taste
- 2 dill pickles, chopped
- 1 tablespoon steak sauce
- 2 teaspoons spicy brown mustard
- 3 tablespoons tomato paste
- 1 head Romaine lettuce, chopped
- 6 cherry tomatoes, sliced in half

Method:

1. Add oil to a pan over medium heat.
2. Cook bacon until golden and crispy.
3. Transfer to a plate covered with paper towels to drain fat.
4. Chop into small bits.
5. Add beef to the same pot and cook for 8 minutes, stirring frequently.
6. Transfer the beef to a soup pot over medium high heat.
7. Pour in the broth and stir in the rest of the ingredients except the lettuce and tomatoes.
8. Reduce heat and simmer for 25 minutes.
9. Garnish with lettuce, bacon and tomatoes before serving.

Nutritional Value:

- Calories 388
- Total Fat 27.1g
- Saturated Fat 13.0g
- Cholesterol 103mg
- Sodium 729mg

- Total Carbohydrates 7.8g
- Dietary Fiber 2.2g
- Protein 28.2g
- Total Sugars 3g
- Potassium 685mg

Creamy Cauliflower Risotto

Preparation Time: 15 minutes
Cooking Time: 15 minutes
Servings: 4

Ingredients:

- ¼ cup ghee
- ½ onion, chopped
- 1 clove garlic, crushed and minced
- 1 head cauliflower, grated
- 1 cup fresh mushrooms, sliced
- 1 cup Parmesan cheese, grated
- ½ cup heavy whipping cream
- Salt and pepper to taste

Method:

1. Add the ghee to a pan over medium heat.
2. Cook the onion and garlic for 3 minutes.
3. Add the cauliflower. Cook for 3 to 4 minutes.
4. Stir in the mushrooms and cook for another 3 minutes.
5. Stir in the rest of the ingredients.
6. Cook for 5 minutes.
7. Serve with main course.

Nutritional Value:

- Calories 350
- Total Fat 29.8g
- Saturated Fat 18g
- Cholesterol 91mg
- Sodium 653mg
- Total Carbohydrates 11.8g
- Dietary Fiber 4.2g
- Protein 12.1g
- Total Sugars 5g
- Potassium 585mg

Zucchini Fries

Preparation Time: 15 minutes
Cooking Time: 30 minutes
Servings: 4

Ingredients:

- Cooking spray
- 2 eggs
- ¾ cup Parmesan cheese, grated
- 1 tablespoon dried mixed herbs
- Pepper to taste
- 1 teaspoon paprika
- 1 ½ teaspoons garlic powder
- 2 lb. zucchini strips

Method:

1. Preheat your oven to 425 degrees F.
2. Cover your baking pan with foil.
3. Spray the foil with cooking oil.
4. In a bowl, beat the eggs.
5. In another bowl, mix the Parmesan cheese, herbs, pepper, paprika and garlic powder.
6. Dip the zucchini strips in the first bowl with eggs.
7. Dredge with the Parmesan cheese mixture.
8. Place on the baking pan.
9. Bake in the oven for 30 minutes.

Nutritional Value:

- Calories 142
- Total Fat 7.2g
- Saturated Fat 3g
- Cholesterol 95mg
- Sodium 284mg
- Potassium 690mg
- Total Carbohydrates 10.4g
- Dietary Fiber 3.4g
- Protein 11.7g
- Total Sugars 5g

Roasted Cauliflower

Preparation Time: 10 minutes
Cooking Time: 15 minutes
Servings: 4

Ingredients:

- 1 head cauliflower, sliced into florets
- Salt and pepper to taste
- 1 teaspoon mixed herbs
- 3 tablespoons olive oil
- ½ cup Parmesan cheese, grated

Method:

1. Preheat your oven to 450 degrees F.
2. Cover your baking pan with foil.
3. Place the cauliflower on the baking pan.
4. Season with salt, pepper and herbs.
5. Toss in olive oil and sprinkle the cheese on top.
6. Bake in the oven for 15 minutes.

Nutritional Value:

- Calories 171
- Total Fat 13.2g
- Saturated Fat 3g
- Cholesterol 9mg
- Sodium 778mg
- Total Carbohydrates 8.4g
- Dietary Fiber 3.8g
- Protein 6.8g
- Total Sugars 4g
- Potassium 458mg

Tuna Salad

Preparation Time: 20 minutes
Cooking Time: 0 minutes
Servings: 4

Ingredients:

- 12 oz. canned tuna in water, drained
- 12 oz. canned tuna in olive oil, drained
- ¾ cup mayonnaise
- 2 stalks green onion, chopped
- 1 tablespoon lime juice
- ½ onion, chopped
- 2 tablespoons mustard
- Salt and pepper to taste

Method:

1. Combine all the ingredients in a bowl.
2. Mix well.
3. Chill in the refrigerator for 10 minutes before serving.

Nutritional Value:

- Calories 423
- Total Fat 22.8g
- Saturated Fat 4g
- Cholesterol 56mg
- Sodium 1027mg
- Total Carbohydrates 6.2g
- Dietary Fiber 0.9g
- Protein 46.9g
- Total Sugars 3g
- Potassium 472mg

Buffalo Cauliflower

Preparation Time: 10 minutes
Cooking Time: 40 minutes
Servings: 4

Ingredients:

- 1 tablespoon butter
- 2 tablespoons olive oil
- ½ cup Buffalo wing sauce
- 6 cups cauliflower florets
- ¼ cup Parmesan cheese, grated

Method:

1. Preheat your oven to 375 degrees F.
2. Melt the butter in a saucepan over medium low heat.
3. Stir in the oil and Buffalo sauce.
4. Toss the cauliflower in the sauce.
5. Transfer to a baking pan and roast in the oven for 30 minutes.
6. Sprinkle with the Parmesan cheese before serving.

Nutritional Value:

- Calories 164
- Total Fat 11.9g
- Saturated Fat 4g
- Cholesterol 12mg
- Sodium 693mg
- Total Carbohydrates 11.2g
- Dietary Fiber 3.6g
- Protein 5.5g
- Total Sugars 3g
- Potassium 443mg

Chapter 12: Desserts

Brownies

Preparation Time: 10 minutes
Cooking Time: 40 minutes
Servings: 12

Ingredients:

- 2/3 cup coconut oil, divided
- ½ teaspoon baking soda
- ¾ cup cocoa powder
- ½ cup boiling water
- 1 cup stevia sugar
- 2 eggs
- 1 1/3 cups almond flour
- ¼ teaspoon salt
- 1 teaspoon vanilla extract

Method:

1. Preheat your oven to 350 degrees F.
2. Grease your baking pan with a little coconut oil.
3. In a bowl, combine the baking soda and cocoa powder.
4. Stir in half of the coconut oil and water. Mix well.
5. Gradually add the remaining coconut oil and eggs. Mix well.
6. Fold in the flour, salt and vanilla.
7. Pour into the baking pan.
8. Bake for 40 minutes.
9. Let cool before slicing and serving.

Nutritional Value:

- Calories 222
- Total Fat 20.5g
- Saturated Fat 12g
- Cholesterol 31mg
- Sodium 114mg
- Total Carbohydrates 7.5g
- Dietary Fiber 3.3g
- Protein 5g
- Total Sugars 1g
- Potassium 94mg

Cheesecake Cupcakes

Preparation Time: 10 minutes
Cooking Time: 15 minutes
Servings: 12

Ingredients:

- ¼ cup butter, melted
- ½ cup almond meal
- 2 eggs
- 16 oz. cream cheese
- 1 teaspoon vanilla extract
- ¾ cup sweetener

Method:

1. Preheat your oven to 350 degrees F.
2. Line your muffin cups with parchment.
3. Combine butter and almond meal in a bowl.
4. Press mixture into the muffin cuts to form the crust.
5. Beat the rest of the ingredients using an electric mixer.
6. Pour mixture on top of the crust.
7. Bake in the oven for 15 minutes.
8. Refrigerate overnight before serving.

Nutritional Value:

- Calories 204
- Total Fat 20g
- Saturated Fat 11g
- Cholesterol 82mg
- Sodium 151mg
- Total Carbohydrates 2.1g
- Dietary Fiber 0.5g
- Protein 4.9g
- Total Sugars 0g
- Potassium 57mg

Choco Peanut Butter Cups

Preparation Time: 3 hours and 10 minutes
Cooking Time: 5 minutes
Servings: 3

Ingredients:

- 1 cup coconut oil
- ½ cup peanut butter
- 2 tablespoons heavy cream
- 1 tablespoon cocoa powder
- 1 teaspoon liquid stevia
- ¼ teaspoon vanilla extract
- ¼ teaspoon salt
- 1 oz. roasted peanuts, chopped

Method:

1. Add coconut oil to a pan over medium heat.
2. Let it melt for 3 minutes.
3. Stir in the rest of the ingredients except the peanuts.
4. Mix well.
5. Remove from heat.
6. Transfer to muffin cups.
7. Sprinkle peanuts on top.
8. Freeze for 3 hours and serve.

Nutritional Value:

- Calories 246
- Total Fat 26g
- Saturated Fat 17g
- Cholesterol 3mg
- Sodium 89mg
- Total Carbohydrates 3.3g
- Dietary Fiber 1.1g
- Protein 3.4g
- Total Sugars 1g
- Potassium 99mg

Lemon Muffins

Preparation Time: 15 minutes
Cooking Time: 15 minutes
Servings: 8

Ingredients:

- 1/3 cup sweetener
- ¼ cup almond flour
- ¼ cup coconut flour
- 1 tablespoon poppy seeds
- 1 tablespoon lemon zest
- ½ teaspoon baking powder
- ½ teaspoon salt
- 3 eggs
- 3 tablespoons butter
- 2 tablespoons sour cream
- ½ teaspoon vanilla extract
- 2 tablespoons heavy whipping cream

Method:

1. Preheat your oven to 350 degrees F.
2. Grease your muffin pan with oil.
3. Combine all the dry ingredients in a bowl.
4. Beat the eggs using an electric mixer and stir in the rest of the ingredients.
5. Slowly add the dry ingredient mixture.
6. Pour batter into the muffin pan.
7. Bake for 20 minutes.

Nutritional Value:

- Calories 116
- Total Fat 10.7g
- Saturated Fat 5g
- Cholesterol 88mg
- Sodium 240mg
- Total Carbohydrates 5g
- Dietary Fiber 0.8g
- Protein 3.6g
- Total Sugars: 1g
- Potassium 43mg

Cinnamon & Butter Cookies

Preparation Time: 10 minutes
Cooking Time: 12 minutes
Servings: 12

Ingredients:

- 2 cups almond flour
- ½ cup butter, softened
- 1 egg
- ½ cup sweetener
- 1 teaspoon vanilla
- 1 teaspoon ground cinnamon

Method:

1. Preheat your oven to 350 degrees F.
2. Cover your baking pan with parchment paper.
3. Mix all the ingredients in a bowl.
4. Form balls from the mixture.
5. Press down the balls on the pan to create the cookies.
6. Bake in the oven for 15 minutes.
7. Let cool before serving.

Nutritional Value:

- Calories 196
- Total Fat 18.4g
- Saturated Fat 6g
- Cholesterol 36mg
- Sodium 60mg
- Total Carbohydrates 12.7g
- Dietary Fiber 2.3g
- Protein 5g
- Total Sugars: 1g
- Potassium 9mg

Cheesecake Bars

Preparation Time: 10 minutes
Cooking Time: 40 minutes
Servings: 16

Ingredients:

- Cooking spray
- 8 oz. cream cheese
- 5 eggs
- 15 oz. pumpkin puree
- 1 teaspoon vanilla extract
- 1 cup granular sweetener
- 1 teaspoon ground cinnamon
- 1 teaspoon pumpkin pie spice

Method:

1. Preheat your oven to 350 degrees F.
2. Coat your baking pan with oil.
3. Beat the cream cheese on high speed.
4. Stir in the rest of the ingredients.
5. Pour the batter into the baking pan.
6. Bake in the oven for 40 minutes.
7. Let cool before slicing into bars.

Nutritional Value:

- Calories 83
- Total Fat 16.5g
- Saturated Fat 9g
- Cholesterol 74mg
- Sodium 128mg
- Total Carbohydrates 3.3g
- Dietary Fiber 0.9g
- Protein 3.3g
- Total Sugars 1g
- Potassium 94mg

Chocolate Mousse

Preparation Time: 10 minutes
Cooking Time: 10 minutes
Servings: 2

Ingredients:

- 3 oz. cream cheese, softened
- ½ cup heavy cream
- 1 teaspoon vanilla extract
- ¼ cup sweetener
- 2 tablespoons cocoa powder
- ¼ teaspoon salt

Method:

1. Beat the cream cheese using an electric mixer until fluffy.
2. Add the cream and vanilla.
3. Stir in the rest of the ingredients.
4. Beat until fluffy.
5. Chill in the refrigerator before serving.

Nutritional Value:

- Calories 373
- Total Fat 37.6g
- Saturated Fat 23g
- Cholesterol 128mg
- Sodium 227mg
- Total Carbohydrates 6.9g
- Dietary Fiber 1.6g
- Protein 5.4g
- Total Sugars: 1g
- Potassium 234mg

Pecan Cheesecake with Mixed Berries

Preparation Time: 15 minutes
Cooking Time: 40 minutes
Servings: 18

Ingredients:

Crust:

- 1 cup pecans
- ¼ teaspoon ground nutmeg
- 1 teaspoon cinnamon
- 1 teaspoon sweetener
- 2 tablespoons melted butter

Filling:

- 1 egg
- 12 oz. cream cheese
- ½ cup sweetener
- ¼ cup sour cream
- ½ teaspoon vanilla extract
- ¼ cup almond milk (unsweetened)
- 1 tablespoon melted butter

Topping:

- 1 cup frozen mixed berries
- 1 tablespoon sweetener

Method:

1. Preheat your oven to 350 degrees F.
2. Add pecans to a blender to chop finely.
3. Add the nutmeg, cinnamon and sweetener to the blender.
4. Pulse to combine.
5. Transfer mixture to a bowl.
6. Stir in the butter.
7. Press into brownie pan to form the crust.

8. Beat the egg using an electric mixer until fluffy.
9. Gradually add the cream cheese, and then the rest of the filling ingredients.
10. Pour into the pan on top of the crust.
11. Bake in the oven for 35 minutes.
12. Put a small pot over medium low heat.
13. Simmer the berries and sweetener for 5 minutes.
14. Pour the berries on top of the cheesecake and serve.

Nutritional Value:

- Calories 155
- Total Fat 14.3g
- Saturated Fat 6g
- Cholesterol 38mg
- Sodium 78mg
- Total Carbohydrates 11.2g
- Dietary Fiber 1g
- Protein 2.7g
- Total Sugars 0g
- Potassium 80mg

Strawberry Ice Cream

Preparation Time: 50 minutes
Cooking Time: 0 minutes
Servings: 8

Ingredients:

- 5 strawberries, hulled
- 2/3 cup sweetener
- 1 teaspoon lemon juice
- 2 ½ cups heavy whipping cream
- ¼ teaspoon salt
- 2 teaspoons vanilla extract
- ½ cup water
- ½ teaspoon vodka

Method:

1. Process strawberries in a blender.
2. Pulse until pureed.
3. Stir in the rest of the ingredients.
4. Use an ice cream maker and follow the directions for processing the mixture.
5. Transfer to a container and freeze overnight.

Nutritional Value:

- Calories 264
- Total Fat 27.6g
- Saturated Fat 17g
- Cholesterol 102mg
- Sodium 48mg
- Total Carbohydrates 19.3g
- Dietary Fiber 0.2g
- Protein 1.6g
- Total Sugars 1g
- Potassium 76mg

Avocado Dessert

Preparation Time: 2 hours and 10 minutes
Cooking Time: 0 minutes
Servings: 2

Ingredients:

- 1 ripe avocado, sliced into cubes
- ¼ cup heavy whipping cream
- ½ teaspoon liquid stevia
- ¼ teaspoon vanilla extract
- ¼ teaspoon ground cinnamon

Method:

1. In a bowl, mash the avocado and stir in the rest of the ingredients.
2. Refrigerate for 1 to 2 hours before serving.

Nutritional Value:

- Calories 266
- Total Fat 25.7g
- Saturated Fat 9g
- Cholesterol 41mg
- Sodium 18mg
- Total Carbohydrates 9.7g
- Dietary Fiber 6.9g
- Protein 2.6g
- Total Sugars 1g
- Potassium 512mg

Conclusion

Once you get started with your keto diet, you will enjoy many of its amazing benefits. But of course, it's not without hard work. You need to do your part by following the proper diet guidelines, getting regular exercise, and getting enough rest.

After your body adjusts, the initial side effects will wear off, and you'll be on your way to a healthier and slimmer you.

Good luck!

Printed in Great Britain
by Amazon

48236478R00066